MW01602866

Summary

of

Eat Smarter:
Use The Power Of Food To Reboot Your
Metabolism, Upgrade Your Brain,
And Transform Your Life

by
Shawn Stevenson

Chapter Zoom

Note to readers:

This is an unofficial summary & analysis of *Shawn Stevenson*'s *"Eat Smarter: Use The Power Of Food To Reboot Your Metabolism, Upgrade Your Brain, And Transform Your Life"* designed to enrich your reading experience. Buy the original book here:

SCAN ME

and they do not sponsor or endorse our publications. This book is unofficial and unauthorized. It is not authorized, approved, licensed, or endorsed by the aforementioned interests or any of their licensees.

The information in this book has been provided for educational and entertainment purposes only.

The information contained in this book has been compiled from sources deemed reliable and it is accurate to the best of the Author's knowledge; however, the Author cannot guarantee its accuracy and validity and cannot be held liable for any errors or omissions. Upon using the information contained in this book, you agree to hold harmless the author from and against any damages, costs, and expenses, including any legal fees, potentially resulting from the application of any of the information provided by this guide. The disclaimer applies to any damages or injury caused by the use and application, whether directly or indirectly, of any advice or information presented, whether for breach of contract, tort, neglect, personal injury, criminal intent, or under any other cause of action. You agree to accept all risks of using the information presented inside this book.

The fact that an individual or organization is referred to in this document as a citation or source of information does not imply that the author or publisher endorses the information that the individual or organization provided. This is an unofficial summary & analytical review and has not been approved by the original author of the book.

Download Your Free Gift

Before you go any further, why not pick up a free gift from me to you?

Biohacking Secrets – a 12-part video and audio training series to learn to live your best life and claim your personal powers!

Scan the QR-Code to get it before it expires!

https://l.ead.me/chapter-zoom-free-gift

TABLE OF CONTENTS

BOOK SUMMARY OVERVIEW

Funny, intelligent, interactive, and informative; that's the best way to summarize Shawn Stevenson in his latest book. Stevenson compiles most of his thoughts gained through experience and a ton of study to present the reader with facts concerning eating smarter. The book is scientific enough to be read by an intelligent head and simple enough to be understood and enjoyed by an eighth-grader.

The author begins the preface and introduction by taking us through his short history and what led him to this path. Growing up, urbanization and capitalism would dictate the way of life for most people, including the diet. The consequences of this counterfeit diet did not reflect immediately on him until his university years when he started developing complications. He was diagnosed with a degenerative bone disorder and degenerative disk disease at the age of 20. Every physician he visited sadly informed him that his only hope was to live on pain meds and survive with his 80-year-old-like bones until his body gave up. In other words, all hope seemed lost for him.

But wait a minute!

He realized the mistake he had made. All along, he had entrusted his life and health to the hands of doctors who did not necessarily know it all since they were not in his shoes. It was time to take back power and begin searching for answers himself. The tremendous response he got that has led him to this very moment is – we are what we eat.

Food enables us to do everything, including the formation of cells, brain development, processing our thoughts, feelings, and emotions, and every other body process you can conceive. What's more, the food doesn't have to be bitter to be better as most people like to claim. Shawn presents us with a curious and intriguing thought: "Perhaps pleasure in food has been a missing ingredient for most diets resulting in a loss of crucial nutritional benefits."

CHAPTER BY CHAPTER SUMMARIES

SUMMARY OF
SECTION I:

EATING FOR FAT LOSS

SUMMARY OF CHAPTER 1:

MAKE THE CONNECTIONS

Shawn begins by trying to establish a clear link between foods and fats. If fats are indispensable to the body, how do we maintain the right fats and eliminate unwanted ones? The importance of fats in the body cannot be underrated, and fats are basically what prevents you from dying. Nonetheless, it can be quite 'clingy' at times if it goes unregulated. Fat forms the structure of every cell and membrane and holds them together. Next time someone calls 'fat-head,' take it a compliment because it's the reality.

Other roles of fat include aiding in the absorption and utilization of certain nutrients, formation, and functioning of sex hormones, protect us from radical climatic changes by regulating the body's temperatures, and even play a key role in our immune system. How cool is fat? But fats, like most other things in life, come in different flavors.

The 'fat community' most people focus on in weight-loss programs is subcutaneous fat. See that fat right under your skin? Yeap, that's it. It is imperative to create proper communication channels to these fat communities to inform them that it's okay to let go at times. Your body is hardwired to store the extra energy as fat for that 'rainy day' even during plenty. Another fat community that needs to let go of its hold on you is visceral fats. This is located around your belly and is actually what results in pot-bellies, especially in men.

Shawn then shows the benefits of intramuscular fat. These three sets of fat communities store white fat.

Brown fat does the exact opposite – it burns fat and energy hence producing heat. In fat loss, you need to increase the brown fat ratio in your body as it is now known to deplete as you age. Another fat community we will take a look at is beige fat, which has chameleon tendencies – it can act as either brown or white fat depending on different factors.

The chapter concludes with Shawn showing how we accumulate this fat. He turns to the 'caloric' conversation and illustrates why using calories as a measure of energy in food is wrong and has misled many dieters over the decades. Most caloric counts are inaccurate, ignore the complexities of digestion, and are based on estimates.

Other factors to consider include differences in enzyme composition from one person to another, types of foods, and whether they are whole or processed, the food preparation process, as well as your microbiome composition. All these factors affect the caloric absorption process but are not included in your food-packaging caloric equations. So how will you optimize your microbiome to make the most of your body composition in relation to food?

YOUR METABOLIC SWITCHES

Shawn likens the internal mechanisms to a programmable computer system. You need the help of enzymes to catalyze the fat-leaving process. The three principal enzymes required here are:

- Hormone-sensitive lipase (HSL)

- Monoglyceride lipase (MGL)

- Adipose triglyceride lipase (ATGL).

The most easily controlled enzyme and point of our focus is hormone-sensitive lipase. The main opposition in containing these enzymes will come from lipoprotein lipase that does its best to keep fat in. But to get access through the door, the enzymes will have to pass through the gatekeepers: *insulin*, *glucagon*, and *adrenaline*.

The owner of this theater business – the *thyroid gland* – is also a key component responsible for controlling the total metabolic rate. At the command centers, we have the *brain*, the chief commander, and the *gut* that follows the command chain. Now you know how the whole community functions.

With that in mind, let's now look at the amigos who may set the house on fire or cause problems in the metabolic community. We call them amigos since they can also be friendly and rectify the problems caused.

The first amigo is inflammation. Inflammation is 100% essential to your health and, specifically, your immune system. Most people tend to view inflammation as a rascal that needs to be eliminated at all costs. The danger, however, lies when the inflammation process goes overboard. This is catastrophic, especially when it occurs in the gut. Food can be the maniac causing inflammation or the fixer addressing the problem.

Amigo number two is hormone dysfunction. Hormones are the special chemical messengers responsible for communication in all your cellular communities. When things are wrong in the communication line, the hormones will send an overflow of unwanted DMs, warranting a negative response. The leading hormonal players involved in fat loss include insulin, glucagon, cortisol, testosterone, estrogen, human growth hormone, and adrenaline.

Coming in last in our amigos' list is appetite dysregulation. Our culture has trained our biology to be in constant need of food – big chunks of hyper-palatable, highly-processed foods, to be precise. Regulating these appetite hormones is, therefore, a vital piece of the puzzle. Would you believe that your body fat is highly responsible for controlling your appetite? Funny, right?

The hormonal message to quit stockpiling food is sent through leptin. There is a linear relationship between the two – the more body fat present, the more leptin is produced. An excess of leptin leads to leptin resistance in obese cases. Therefore, the brain is unable to receive the message that the system is full of junk. Abnormalities in the microbiome and inflammation are some of the causes of leptin resistance. Another cause is stockpiling our system with sugar, especially highly-concentrated liquid fructose. You want to stay away from sodas just to be on the safe side.

Other potent hormones that need a touch of regulation include peptide YY (PYY), which reduces appetite and lowers the risk of excess body fat storage. Adiponectin moves body fat away from the belly fat region to the subcutaneous fat area. Glucagon-like peptide-1 (GLP-1) increases feelings of satiety and stabilizes blood sugar. Neuropeptide Y (NPY) is an appetite-stimulating compound found in the brain; cholecystokinin (CCK), involved in digestion and appetite regulation. These are the master players ruling your system.

It's now time to tap into your fat-burning potential.

FAT LOSS ESSENTIAL # 1: SUPPORT YOUR MICROBIOME

The next three chapters shed light on the three essentials needed to maintain long-term fat loss. Most diets will work for some people for a short duration only. The right knowledge will enable you to sustain the lost fat for a long time regardless of the diet you subscribe to.

Your microbiome is a stalwart tool and acts as the foundation of your metabolism. To model the microbiome community, you need to diversify your food intake.

Blueberries and pistachios, for instance, are now known to improve and diversify your microbiome and overall bifidobacteria ratio. Occasionally swap in other berries for better results. As much as possible, allow your diet to sync in with changes in seasons. Eating foods that are in season is one sure way to introduce diversity to your microbiome. Additionally, include vegetables and mixed fruits to minimize the growth of pathogenic bacteria population significantly.

Humanity is known to have different tastes and preferences for a lot of things, especially food. Similarly, your bacteria also has a tongue for different flavors.' To keep them happy and healthy, try adding apples and pears that are rich in pectin. Other prebiotic foods include an occasional Jerusalem artichoke, asparagus, garlic, onions, chicory roots, and jicama. Leeks, citrus, and bananas will boost your fructooligosaccharides content. High-quality cocoa-rich chocolates will also do you justice if you cannot find the actual cocoa seeds.

To improve and support your microbiome, you also need to focus on increasing your fiber content for both soluble and insoluble fibers. To achieve a high soluble fiber content, consider foods such as flaxseeds, carrots, Brussels sprouts, black beans, nectarines, pears, avocados, apples, broccoli, and sweet potatoes. Insoluble fiber can be sourced from cocoa, spinach, okra beans, berries, lentils, whole grains, almonds, walnuts, and once again, *APPLES.* See why they concluded that an apple a day is going to keep that needle away?

Insoluble fiber is known to trigger satiety by influencing the mechanoreceptors in your gut hence deactivating the hunger hormones. Moreover, fiber is commonly known to help in removing metabolic wastes and excess estrogen. All these factors make insoluble fibers a must-have component for a robust microbiome.

Another classification of fibers that is quickly gaining recognition among the scientific community is resistant starch. Resistant starch helps keep you 'full' and adds a ton of other benefits. Some rich sources of resistant starch include green bananas, cashews, white yams, white beans, oats, corn, and potato starch. If you are attentive, you might have noticed the color of all these foods – white, yellow, or beige. This is to say that the food color is a useful marker and indicator of the nutritional content found in that particular food.

A good number of people today are wheat averse because of the way modern diets have demonized wheat. These diets ignore wheat and other grains because of gluten in them; hence the masses have also developed an instinctive and irrational fear. This has led to every food package having a 'gluten-free' stamp on it, including water bottles! This misinformation has developed at the expense of certain nutrients that are relatively rare in other foods. Shawn shows how it is useless to religiously follow any diet to the detriment of one's health. The reader should note that the method of preparation and storage of such foods also matters. For example, if properly stored, white and brown rice will give you all the fiber benefits minus the associated risks.

Having taken a look at prebiotics and fibers and their role in supporting a friendly flora in your microbiome, let's now take a dive and assess some probiotic foods and see how they are also essential to your overall health.

Kimchi is quickly gaining popularity even outside its homeland, Korea, and for good reasons. A close cousin to kimchi is sauerkraut. Both of these are healthier and more nutritious varieties of cabbages rich in extra vitamins and minerals. Sauerkraut also produces lactobacillus – a potent probiotic known to accelerate fat loss.

Are you a yogurt fan? Drink some more and keep your microbiome smiling till you are grey. Non-dairy varieties of yogurt include coconut-milk and oat-milk based yogurt. The same also applies to traditionally prepared soybeans (though fermentation) to remove the lectins. A regular light touch of kombucha (fermented black tea) will have your microbiome throwing the party of the year. Pickling is a suitable method of food preservation and mostly relies on fermentation.

A healthier upgrade to conventional soda is kefir – a probiotic, fermented drink that also works wonders. Traditional communities were commonly known to use fermentation, and now we see why it is such a smart tool for your microbiome.

Now you know how to ignite your microbiome!

SUMMARY OF CHAPTER 4:

FAT LOSS ESSENTIAL # 2: MIND YOUR MACROS

Generally, when addressing macros, there are three big guys and two lesser guys we need to pay attention to. The first big guy we need to tackle is ***protein***. Most dieticians are known to underrate the significance of proteins. Shawn, however, presents us with a completely different picture.

Proteins have incredible benefits, including feelings of satiety and aiding in the digestion process. Aim at increasing your protein ratio in relation to carbohydrates and fats. However, an overcharge is more or less similar to pressing the kill switch on your liver and kidneys. Our protein requirements increase as we get older. If possible, keep the percentage at 30% of your total macros if your goal is fat loss. Alternatively, you can determine your protein needs based on your body weight. Other factors to consider include gender, location, and daily physical activity. That said, your body should be the base marker of the quantity of protein you ingest.

The quality of the protein also plays a massive role in the kind of nutrients gained. Most livestock bearers feed their animals with antibiotics to increase the animal's total production for animal-based proteins. However, this makes the animal 'sicker' for human consumption. Stevenson comes up with a quote that makes logical sense when referring to animal protein, "You are what you eat ate!"

Please note that every plant also has a fraction of protein quantity that differs from plant to plant. Some good sources for vegans and vegetarians' protein include milk (which may keep the three amigos at bay), eggs, beans, peas, black beans, and lentils. Sprouted soybeans, tofu, natto, and tempeh also fall in this protein-rich category.

Nuts and seeds have higher fat content and should thus be taken sparingly. Almonds are especially beneficial before meals. Opt for uncooked or dehydrated varieties when it comes to nuts since these still have their high nutrient-content intact. Other nuts with remarkable protein benefits include walnuts, hazelnuts, Brazil nuts, and pecans.

Hemp seeds top the protein charts when analyzing sources rich in this macronutrient. Hemp seeds have an upward of up to 30% protein content. Pumpkin seeds are also rich in proteins and other minerals and are a good source when fighting obesity. Do not leave out flaxseeds behind.

Still, want more non-animal sources of protein? Consider adding spirulina and its blue-green algae companions. These algae varieties are loaded with high-quality protein percentage plus other nutrients not common in conventional plants. Spirulina is closely related to chlorella, which has an abundance of chlorophyll and is amazingly potent in weight loss regimes. These algae give you the control that manufacturers of hyper-palatable foods took away from you, enabling you to control your appetite. The last algae Shawn recommends is Aphanizomenon flos-aquae (AFA).

According to many nutritionists, grains should not be consumed in large quantities but should only act as a complementary protein source. The best sources here include oats, quinoa, and amaranth. Amaranth has all the protein benefits, plus it just so happens to be gluten-free and prevents inflammatory precursors.

If protein powder is used, the reader should only use it to supplement whole protein foods. Always aim for the real stuff if you are to enjoy quality nutrition.

Carbohydrates are the second big team player in your macronutrient list. Carbs play a pivotal role in the game and can bring in significant wins or lead to unforgettable losses. Taking in the right type of carbs is therefore crucial to up your game. To achieve the right game stats, you first need to identify your body's carbohydrate tipping point. Remember that your microbiome is unique, and thus, this point will differ from one person to another.

That said, an easy trick to arrive at this point would be to start by reducing the daily carbs intake to 100 grams. Slowly work your way up from this point as you monitor your energy levels, cravings, hunger between meals, general focus, and sleep quality and patterns.

Findings show that there is no one-size-fits-all type of diet because of variations in the microbiome, genetics, ethnicity, and even age. This means that for an efficient metabolism, you need not constrain yourself to one particular diet. Another exciting factor often ignored is that *a macro is not merely a macro*, as most people assume. The same amount of macros in a cookie may result in an utterly different response from the same amount of macros in a banana.

Talking of bananas, the reader should be careful on fructose intake (not to be confused with high fructose corn syrup, which is bad business for your microbiome). Aim for a higher intake of less sugary fruits such as berries, squash, pumpkin, cucumbers, tomatoes, avocados, olives, and eggplants.

Fruits and vegetables increase the rate of fat loss, protect against weight gain and obesity, and reduce waist circumference. These have healthy carbohydrates, which should change how you look at carbohydrates.

Smart eating dictates that you should observe the right timing in carbs consumption for the best metabolic response. Shawn suggests having carbs during dinner when going to bed since your digestion will go on defense and use the carbs rather than stored fats. Consuming carbs in the morning may make you hungrier and lead you to snack some more. The same logic applies to carbs and exercise: take your carbohydrates after a workout for the best fat loss results. Also, be sure to add leafy greens and other non-starchy vegetables as the lion's share in your food servings, including breakfast.

FATS!

For the longest time, fats had received an inferior label and a nasty reputation until the early 2000s. A study in 2002 emerged to save the guy who had been silent all along the defamation years. The Harvard study showed that *dietary fat is not body fat*. Nevertheless, to this day, people still confuse the two.

To heal the broken relationship between humanity and dietary fat, we will have to understand the personality and different types of dietary fats. We might even need a change of names to say dietary oils or dietary lipids, or better still, *'fexties'* (fats+sexies = smart, right?).

Saturated fats are the first type and are known to reduce coronary heart disease risk and lead to longevity! However, the source and type of food where saturated fats are derived is of great importance. Surprisingly, saturated fats will also decrease the overall body fat mass, reduce inflammatory cytokines, and increase lean (muscle) mass. How on earth can the villain called saturated fats do all that?

When considering fats, aim for short-chain and medium-chain fats for the best nutritional results.

Monounsaturated fats are less stable than saturated fats. However, with proper preparation and storage, they are sure to return the benefits minus most of the detriments. Some rich sources include olive oil, beef, avocados, butter, nuts, and seeds. You are probably aware of these sources but have you tried out omega-7?

You cannot possibly underrate the importance of omega-7. Some great sources include wild-caught cold fish sardines, sea bass, salmon, macadamia nuts, sea buckthorn, berry oil, and avocados.

Omega-9s are more common, and the best-known source is olive oil. Sunflower seeds and oil, avocado oil, almonds, and macadamia nuts are additional sources of omega-9.

The more the bends in the fat formation, the more unstable the fats are. This is the case with polyunsaturated fats, which have more bends hence more unstable molecules. They include omega-6 and omega-3 fats, and fish oils just happen to be a superb source.

Plant sources of polyunsaturated fats include flaxseeds, chia seeds, kale, walnuts, hemp seeds, and purslane. Alternatively, you can source out algae oils, which is where fish derive this essential nutrient from. What's most important is to stabilize the ratio between omega-6 and omega-3.

Remember the two small guys on the team? Well, the first we need to look at is alcohol. Once alcohol steps into the picture, the burning of body fat, glucose, and other dietary macros come to a halt. The type of alcohol also makes a big difference as some have added sugars making the liquor more harmful and addictive.

Red wine is highly prized due to the presence of resveratrol and antioxidants. 1½ glasses a day will bring in the much needed fat loss results. Going beyond this level may be detrimental to your fat-loss progress.

Finally, we have water! The most neglected macronutrient of all. Study shows that water triggers lipolysis (release of stored body fat) and increases the metabolic rate through water-induced thermogenesis. Water is also known to maintain your DNA and maintain blood integrity, create lymph fluid, regulate body temperatures, create cerebrospinal fluid for your central nervous system, among other neglected duties.

Most importantly, water enables a proper and fluent communication flow between hormones and neurotransmitters throughout the body. In other words, don't stay dehydrated at all costs. An excess of water is also harmful and problematic to your metabolism.

Be cautious about the quality of water. The best sources are spring water, well water, or distilled water that has been remineralized.

So how much water is enough? As with the other nutrients, simply listen to your body's demands. Otherwise, you can use a simple formula Shawn gives. Take your total body weight in pounds and divide by 2 to find your baseline daily water content. If you weigh 300 pounds, your daily baseline water quantity is 150 ounces.

Always have your water bottle with you as often as possible and drink a glass or two first thing you wake up. Avoid plastic bottles and opt for steel.

SUMMARY OF CHAPTER 5:

FAT LOSS ESSENTIAL # 3: OPTIMIZE HORMONE FUNCTION

Now that you are equipped with the right macronutrient knowledge, having a proper understanding of micronutrients will empower you to maximize the acquired information.

Proper functioning of the hormones hugely depends on the flexibility of the mitochondria. Statistics now show that 56% of the American populace is magnesium deficient – a key player in healthy mitochondria. Some rich sources include avocados, almonds, and spinach, which eventually reduce the risk of type 2 diabetes and insulin resistance.

The micronutrients we will be shedding light on include minerals, vitamins, enzymes, trace minerals, antioxidants, polyphenols, carotenoids, just to mention but a few. When these are combined with the macronutrients in proper quantities, your genetic expression will be well on its way to seventh heaven.

This leads us to *epigenetics*, which teaches about the diverse factors (such as environment and stress), which may influence our genes. Shawn gives a stronger warning on what he has already reiterated in the book: turn to whole foods/real foods if you want to take back control of your genetic fate, or else your genes (what you eat) will control you.

Consider these foods as complements to your micronutrients needs:

- Salubrious fruits include blueberries known to be rich in flavonoids that prevent weight gain and inflammation. Blueberries are also rich in vitamin C and K. Opt for wild-harvested blueberries or the fresh and frozen organic variety.

- Fresh organic cherries possess anthocyanins that shrink fat cells and reduce the expression of inflammatory genes.

- Nuts and seeds not only have fiber and healthy fats in attractive amounts but also have distinct micronutrients. Nutritious sources include acorns, hazelnuts, chestnuts, apple seeds, watermelon seeds, and pumpkin seeds. Almonds and cacao beans (found in dark chocolate) will add vitality to your gut flora and improve your metabolism while reducing clostridia, which leads to fat gain.

- Eggs, especially the yolk, are loaded with nutrients that can lower the ghrelin hunger hormones. They are rich in vitamin B12, zinc, choline, and vitamin D. Examples include chicken eggs, duck eggs, quail eggs, and turkey eggs.

- Wild-caught fish is a prime source of vitamin B12, iodine, and potassium. Excellent examples include red snapper, tilapia, and sole.

- Seaweeds are conventionally used in medicine, during ceremonies, and for food. Kelp, for instance, is necessary to make thyroid hormones T3 and T4. Kelp has more calcium content than most known land veggies. Close kelp relatives include dulse (packed with magnesium), hijiki, wakame, arame, sea lettuce, and nori, which have immense potassium levels, selenium, zinc, B-vitamins, and other necessary micronutrients.

- Drinks to add to your routine include black tea, green tea, and coffee (morning hours to avoid sleep problems.) Remember, the quality is of great importance to the derived micronutrients.

- By now, you probably have a hella lot of respect for veggies – especially the greener varieties. Kales have satiety hormones and are known to lower the waist circumference. Use either extra virgin olive oil or coconut oil for cooking these veggies. Green veggies spark the release of adiponectin, GLP-1, and CCK. They include Swiss chard, spinach, romaine lettuce, bok choy, mustard greens, collard greens, green leaf lettuce, and arugula. The list is endless.

- Cruciferous veggies also have micronutrients that will be highly beneficial. They include cauliflowers, rutabagas, Brussel sprouts, and broccoli.

- Spice your life for a spicier microbiome. Turmeric has anti-inflammatory and anti-obesity effects due to the presence of curcumin. On the other hand, Ginger has zingerone found to stimulate the activity of the HSL (you did not forget about Mr. hormone-sensitive lipase, did you?) and increase fat breakdown. A teaspoon of natural salt a day will ensure you enjoy the right amounts of sodium in your system, translating to proper fluid balance, modulating blood pressure and muscle contractions, and conducting impulses in the nervous system.

- Medium-chain triglycerides (MCT Oils) will lead to faster digestion and generally have a muscle-sparing effect. Don't overdo it, though.

SUMMARY OF
SECTION II:

EATING FOR MENTAL PERFORMANCE, BETTER
RELATIONSHIPS, AND BETTER SLEEP

BRAIN GAMES

The human brain can be considered the most complicated object in the known universe and one of the most delicate. Because of its delicate nature, the Creator included blood-brain barriers (BBB) – a complicated series of a state-of-the-art security system. Shawn explains that the BBB is hardwired to allow some nutrients and prevent anything it will consider as a pathogen, toxin, or any dangerous compound.

For the best brain performance, we all need neuro-nutrition data to feed this powerful organ – and we need to provide it the right stuff.

For starters, water containing the right electrolytes tops the list of your neuro-nutrition as the most significant part of your brain is formed of water. These electrolytes in water (such as sodium and magnesium) help send electrical signals throughout the brain cells, restore brain plasticity, and improve cognitive functioning. You don't want to keep yourself on thirst-mode as it enhances fatigue and makes easy tasks appear to be rocket science.

Closely behind water, we have fat as the next principal brain constituent, comprising roughly 11% of the brain's dry weight. The fat category in your brain is called structural fats. These provide cellular structure and technical support. To boost the structural fats, consider upping your omega intake, as discussed in chapter 4. Omega-3s will introduce phospholipids into your command center that provides cellular communication.

A new study shows promising results in using MCT oils to address Alzheimer's at its infancy stages while improving cognitive impairment. MCTs may provide both direct and indirect brain fuel source. Sources include cow and goat's milk, coconut oils, and concentrated amounts in coffee, smoothies, salads, and more.

With that in mind, how do we promote brain hygiene?

Turmeric gives your brain 'virtual spa treatment'. It's known to reduce brain inflammations, excavates heavy metals, and slows down the aging of neurons. This treatment leads to improved memory functioning, neuroplasticity, and stimulates the creation of new brain cells.

Walnuts have the potential of reducing oxidative stress, inflammation, and protects your brain cells from an early demise.

Cinnamon lowers oxidative stress, improves the health of neurons, and learning speed.

Consuming sugars in large amounts is relative to casting a grenade at your command center. It increases the risk of Alzheimer's, stroke, dementia, and what medics now call 'type 3 diabetes.' Make sure your sugar intake does not supersede your carbohydrate tipping point. Sugars also increase the chances of getting cancer and ruin your microbiome.

Other dangers include being underweight and malnourished, as it will significantly reduce your brain size. Similarly, the larger the waist size, the smaller the brain gets – precisely, the gray matter in the brain shrinks. This region is responsible for muscle functions, self-control, and sensory perception.

SUMMARY OF CHAPTER 7:

FOOD LOVE LANGUAGE

The food we eat affects our relationships and community at large. Shawn presents a couple of studies to cement this correlation. In other words, food can be a powerful tool of healing and happiness or a potent weapon of degradation and disease.

Studies show that eating together as a family influences healthier food choices in children's lives and fewer sodas and processed foods. Having TVs switched off more often leads to less consumption of junk, including soda and chips.

Family meals also lower stress at work and boost productivity and employee morale. Parents' absenteeism is now seen to contribute considerably to the malnourished physical, emotional, and spiritual health of the family and community.

Increased working hours have also resulted in higher levels of anxiety, depression, and chronic diseases. Start by scheduling weekly meals together, including seniors who are often left out of the equation.

Marketing and advertising of low-quality foods have led to more production of this type of food due to demand elasticity. The government has also played a HUGE role in promoting these obese-prone foods (mostly intentionally) by subsidizing them. Lower-income communities have thus suffered the full wrath of the obesity pandemic in America.

Find ways for you to be the force to drive the change. Engage in community events and organizations that fight for such causes in your community. Direct your taxpayer's money to higher-food standards and lifestyle. Your dollar is a sure way to inform the policymakers of what you want to see. It's one way to make your voice audible against a crude system.

Use food to speak the five love languages and develop more meaningful relationships. Maximize the value of food to spend time with others and offer personalized gifts to loved ones. Well prepared real foods can also make an intimate physical touch or come as an act of service. Further, still, you take the opportunity to offer words of affirmation during meal times with friends, colleagues, and family.

SUMMARY OF CHAPTER 8:

EDIBLE SLEEP

Both rapid eye movement (REM sleep) and deep sleep play a crucial role in consolidating what we learn daily into our short and long-term memories. Additionally, quality sleep enhances procedural (skills and procedures) and declarative memory (recall and facts).

The benefits of quality sleep aren't felt by the brain alone, as your immune system and the entire microbiome reap the rewards. Immunological memory is now known to develop during sleep: this allows our bodies to recall former pathogens and the body's response. Moreover, sleep helps fortify your body's defense against chronic diseases.

Your genetic expression, which determines everything from your skin to body composition, also heavily relies on your sleep quality. So precisely how does food come into the picture?

Remember how food affects your microbiome, as discussed in chapter 3? Well, your gut health is also influenced by sleep-related hormones and neurotransmitters mostly found in the gut. A good example is serotonin, which is used to make melatonin. This means that a healthy microbiome is the root of your sleep wellness and vice versa.

To achieve that, keep away from:

- ✗ Agricultural chemicals
- ✗ Artificial sweeteners and excessive sugars
- ✗ Alcohol, especially during bedtime
- ✗ Coffee close to bedtime
- ✗ Haphazard or repeated antibiotics
- ✗ High-stress levels
- ✗ Chlorinated water
- ✗ Lack of exercise and movement
- ✗ Chemical food additives and preservatives.

Expose yourself to the following nutrients:

- ✓ Calcium – Boosts REM and deep sleep and present in spinach, kale, collard greens, lentils, beans, chia seeds, almonds, and sesame.
- ✓ Tryptophan – One of the nine essential amino acids richly sourced from chicken, turkey, eggs, cheese, tofu, spinach, pumpkin seeds, peanuts, and spirulina.
- ✓ Vitamin C – found in superfoods such as camu camu berries, amla berries, and acerola berries. Other familiar sources include papaya, citrus fruits, green leafy veggies, strawberries, broccoli, bell peppers, and kiwifruit.
- ✓ Vitamin D – freely available from the sun and in food sources such as sardines, cod liver oil, egg yolk, and culinary mushrooms.
- ✓ Potassium – Found in green leafy veg, sea veggies, black and white beans, salmon, yogurt, and avocados.
- ✓ Magnesium – Excellent sources include tofu, leafy greens, fatty fish, dark chocolate, black beans, and almonds.
- ✓ Omega-3s.

✓ Extra accessories that should work as supplements include chamomile, mushroom reishi, valerian, L-theanine, and melatonin supplements.

SUMMARY OF
SECTION III:

THE SCIENCE OF MEAL TIMING AND
THE EAT SMARTER 30-DAY PROGRAM

SUMMARY OF CHAPTER 9:

FOOD O'CLOCK

Shawn introduces the aspect of timing as the final eat smart strategy. He suggests ***intermittent fasting,*** which isn't a new invention.

Our genome is created to favor survival in an environment characterized by periods of feast and famine. However, modern-day humans are constantly 'nibbling' on food or *snacking,* as it's commonly called. This means the microbiome has more time for storing up fat upon fat and lesser time to burn the fat.

Intermittent fasting flips the metabolic switch that shifts metabolism from fat creation and fat storage to mobilization of body fat in the form of free fatty acids and fatty acid-derived ketones used as fuel. In simpler terms, your body presses the switch button from storing fat to actually using it. The process places glucagon in the driver's seat while simultaneously improving insulin sensitivity.

The benefits of intermittent fasting include:

- Enhancing satiety hormones

- Supports fat loss

- Retention of lean muscle mass

- Improve overall brain health by stimulating the formation of new brain cells via increased levels of *brain-derived neurotrophic factor (BDNF)*

- Increases melatonin concentration in the gut and brain, thus better sleep

- Lower risks of diseases

- Slows the aging process

Aim to come up with your personalized blocks of time when you are eating and not eating. Don't do it so religiously though, at the expense of family meals, events, good times, hunger, or even a date!

SUMMARY OF CHAPTER 10:

PRE-GAME: SMARTER TOOLS FOR LASTING SUCCESS

The final chapter concludes with a 30-day program to get you started. Here, Shawn provides a comprehensive strategy of executing the eat smart goals talked of throughout the book. The recipes are alluring and easy to make and combine all the foods spoken of previously.

Shawn gives his **F.A.S.T**. transformation tips to set the ball of implementation rolling:

- **F:** Figure out your ideal eating and fasting windows.
- **A:** Adjust this to fit your lifestyle by:
  - Being consistent but neurotic,
  - Knowing the difference between hunger and habit,
  - Keeping the basics in mind.
- **S:** Safeguard your results with supportive nutrition such as coffee, green tea, rooibos tea, and MCT oils.

- **T:** Track your goals of how you look, feel, and perform by taking note of:

    - your hunger and cravings,

    - your sleep quality,

    - your overall digestion,

    - and your energy levels throughout the day.

Now you are fully armed to lead an intelligent life with the eat smarter plan by Shawn Stevenson.

BACKGROUND INFORMATION ABOUT EAT SMARTER

Eat Smarter is a nutrition book solely focused on you – the reader. Unlike most nutrition books that limit the dieter within specific confines, *Eat Smarter* opens the door for you to develop a personalized plan that works for you. Shawn gives evidence why this strategy is so effective, indicating how diverse the human microbiome is from one person to another. Shawn uses an engaging and interactive approach to reach the mind and connect with the reader. He uses everyday-examples to make intricate scientific details relatable to any reader.

Eat Smarter gives you the power to take back control of poor eating habits and revolutionize your health. With this in your hands, you can reverse certain diseases that doctors term as 'incurable.' Essentially, 'you are what you eat,' and it's high time to develop smarter food choices.

BACKGROUND INFORMATION ABOUT SHAWN STEVENSON

Shawn Stevenson is the host and author of the # 1 top trending health podcast in the U.S. – *The Model Health Show.* He is a graduate of the University of Missouri, having studied business, biology, and nutritional sciences. He is also an author of *Sleep Smarter: 21 Essential Strategies to Sleep Your Way to a Better Body, Better Health, and Bigger Success.* He went ahead and became the founder of Advanced Integrative Health Alliance, offering global nutritional services to organizations as well as individuals. His success and popularity in the nutrition community are also evident in multiple magazines and major media outlets. Shawn is also a family man with a lovely wife who has been a major part of his journey.

TRIVIA QUESTIONS

1. Why does Shawn suggest a complete name change of dietary fats?

2. "We are what we eat ate!" How is this statement reflective of our society and eating habits today?

3. Which are the three amigos who may jeopardize your community and still rectify problems?

4. Why can't our bodies function without inflammation occurring?

5. What is the color of food supposed to tell you?

6. Why is it dangerous to religiously follow any given diet?

7. Manufacturers have developed hyper-palatable foods that have robbed you of your right to eat healthier. True or false?

8. How does Shawn explain epigenetics?

9. How can you use food to exercise the five love languages?

10. What is your strategy to execute the plan to eat smarter?

Thank You

We would like to thank you very much for supporting us and reading through to the end. We know you could have picked any number of books to read, but you picked this book and for that we are extremely grateful.

We hope you enjoyed your reading experience. If so, it would be really nice if you could share this book with your friends and family by posting to Facebook and Twitter.

Chapter Zoom stands for the highest reading quality and we will always endeavor to provide you with high-quality books.

Would you mind leaving us a review on Amazon before you go? It will mean a lot to us and support us in creating high-quality guidelines for you in the future.

Thanks once again and here's where you can leave a review:

Warmly yours,

The Chapter Zoom Team

Made in the USA
Coppell, TX
22 January 2021

48612813R00036